Christine's new book, *The Resilient Leader*, is a phenomenal book on how we can all learn from incredibly difficult and challenging situations, turn them into positives, and then apply those lessons to everyday life. A must for anyone going through turbulent times!

So often, many of us use our previous life lessons to navigate through the challenges ahead of us. None have done that more powerfully than Perakis. In her book *The Resilient Leader*, she shows us the invaluable lessons she uncovered through her experiences—highly useful and extremely necessary to win big in business today.

Perakis shares the valuable resilience strategies that helped her survive two Category 5 hurricanes to show us how we can prepare for and endure the catastrophic events that inevitably occur in business and in life. I know I am sleeping better after having read her amazing story, and I'm the Sleep Doctor!

—**MICHAEL J. BREUS**, PhD, The Sleep Doctor, international bestselling author

None of us needs to feel whipped around by the inevitable tumultuous events in our businesses. Perakis offers up the Seven Barometers of Resilience—practical strategies that we can implement before catastrophe strikes in our lives or business.

—**MARK GOULSTON**, MD, bestselling author of *Just Listen*

As an executive in my young company, Christine helped me become a leader in my industry. Now, she compiles the manifold skills that she has honed over her lifetime—as an attorney, boat captain, business owner, executive coach, and survivor of two Category 5 hurricanes—into a road map for weathering even the worst of personal and professional setbacks, emerging as a winner.

— **KEVIN GOETZ**, founder/CEO of Screen Engine/ASI

A must-read for all, not just for business owners. Christine's experience of survival captures the maturity needed to be able to fight back and survive any of life's catastrophes, valuable life lessons to develop the inner strength to thrive and win in challenging situations. In today's era of entrepreneurship, most creating or seeking to attract the lives they desire do so without a solid plan to succeed. *The Resilient Leader* shows what it takes to build the character of a successful leader—able to plan, prepare, and have the ability to stay strong and change strategy as needed without letting fear paralyze or stops us.

—**LIZET ZAYAS**, entrepreneur, founder of Successfuly and host of *Successfuly Stories*

Perakis uses valuable resilience strategies, gained during her survival of two Category 5 hurricanes, to demonstrate how anyone can properly prepare and endure inevitable circumstances that arise in business and life.

—**KEN RUTKOWSKI**, super connector, entrepreneur, international speaker

Over and above its mission to deliver actionable advice, the surprise here is what a great story it tells: an edge-of-your-seat view from the eye of the storm and the revelations to come.

—**DARLENE WINTER**, entrepreneur, investor

THE RESILIENT LEADER

Life-Changing Strategies to Overcome Today's Turmoil and Tomorrow's Uncertainty

CHRISTINE PERAKIS, ESQ.

Photo Credits
Internal images © page vi, Miguel Navarro/Getty Images; page x, VichoT/Getty Images;
page xvi, Westend61/Getty Images; page 2, NASA/SPL/Getty Images; page 10,
Christophe Launay/Getty Images; page 20, Oleh_Slobodeniuk/Getty Images; page 28,
SONGPHOL THESAKIT/Getty Images; page 36, 73, 120, Hero Images/Getty Images;
page 38, FangXiaNuo/Getty Images; page 50, Colin Anderson Productions pty ltd/Getty
Images; page 54, CasarsaGuru/Getty Images; page 62, iceninephoto/Getty Images;
page 65, AlenaPaulus/Getty Images; page 74, Klaus Vedfelt/Getty Images; page 86,
MathieuRivrin/Getty Images; page 91, esemelwe/Getty Images; page 94, James O'Neil/
Getty Images; page 96, EXTREME-PHOTOGRAPHER/Getty Images; page 104, Tom
Merton/Getty Images; page 106, Till Findl / EyeEm/Getty Images; page 108, pixdeluxe/
Getty Images; page 116, Caiaimage/Tom Merton/Getty Images; page 126, Alexander W
Helin/Getty Images
Internal images on pages xiv, 32, 42, 58, 66, 84, 114, and 128 have been provided by
Unsplash or Pixabay; these images are licensed under CC0 Creative Commons and have
been released by the author for use.

Published by Simple Truths, an imprint of Sourcebooks
P.O. Box 4410, Naperville, Illinois 60567-4410
(630) 961-3900
sourcebooks.com

Printed and bound in Singapore.
OGP 10 9 8 7 6 5 4 3 2 1

To the resilient and beloved people of the BVI who helped me weather the hurricanes, my fellow storm survivors who gave me shelter, strength, and support, and Category 5 "storm" survivors everywhere.

CONTENTS

PROLOGUE
HOW DID I GET HERE?

"All you need in this life is ignorance and confidence, and then success is sure."

—MARK TWAIN

Many of us have encountered a Category 5 storm—whether the "storm" is launching and growing a business, drowning in debt, having the roof blow off a relationship, or actual flooding in the streets. Even prior to the calamitous events that inspired *The Resilient Leader*, I was no stranger to extreme Category

5–level events. Starting, growing, and expanding ten businesses of my own; helping hundreds of others do the same on five continents; navigating boats across oceans; and enduring heartbreak, extreme financial distress, and several other natural disasters—like devastating earthquakes and fires—are the kinds of "storms" I have grown adept at weathering.

Despite my experiences with natural and other disasters, I never gave much thought to hurricanes before moving to the Caribbean. I'm from California, where people move *for* the weather. I have had a lot of experience and training in navigating the elements. I was a professional rescuer on the mountains and at sea; a one-hundred-ton-boat captain responsible for steering people through all kinds of weather and potential actual disaster. I also spent my career guiding others through their own business challenges as a lawyer, strategic business advisor, entrepreneur, and C-suite executive. I was confident I could handle anything... Then I found myself all alone in the middle of the most powerful storm to ever strike the Atlantic Basin; it was tearing relentlessly through the British Virgin Islands, my adopted island-nation. In those first terrifying moments, I had to wonder, *What in the world am I doing here, alone in this storm?* I should have had a better plan for my own life's catastrophes. Everything I thought I could rely on was blown away with my roof: I had to reinvent who I was to **survive**.

In the darkest hours of the first hurricane experience, I grasped that my tendency to isolate myself when things were tough or uncomfortable kept me behind an impervious wall that jeopardized my life in the storm. I am certain that there are others who find themselves disempowered, isolated, mindlessly "going it alone" in their own Category 5 storms. I want to share with you the tools I uncovered to thrive no matter what challenges you face. No one should ever be buried alive by circumstances beyond their control. Our salvation, competence, confidence, and **empowerment** to get through—as I discovered the

hard way—depend on the ability to become our own rescuer, a **Storm Warrior**.

Anyone who has experienced the "storms" of life—business, money, career, family, or natural disasters—is a Cat 5 survivor. Becoming a Storm Warrior is the difference between being a victim and using these forces to flourish. My habitual behavior put my life in danger in that first hurricane; I was defenseless against its power. With the storm's grip on me in the darkness, trapped in my shelter, I could either give up or learn from my mistakes, so I and others would never find themselves alone in a Category 5 "storm."

Once the winds died down, leaving me to fend for myself in a post-apocalyptic landscape, I discovered what it would take to get me through the experience to thrive. I learned how being of service could turn strangers into community as well as how critical communication was to my survival. Most of all, I came to accept that I could not handle a Category 5 situation alone. I had to learn how to ask for help fast, because a second

Cat 5 hurricane hit exactly two weeks later. In the aftermath, I turned the most terrifying and traumatic experience of my life into one that allowed me to flourish on my island for those months and beyond—my world changed forever.

I've often been asked, "Why did you stay?" On some level, I knew that being on island was purposeful. Although my first answer was always "I felt fully prepared," I couldn't explain it beyond that. Being there, I could protect my property prior to, during, and in the aftermath of the storms. I thought, *How bad could it get?* I had the gold standard of hurricane protection—galvanized metal panels screwed into the walls of the building with concrete screws to cover my windows and doors. I'd been offshore in gale force winds before. I wasn't afraid of weather, especially considering my preparedness. I am, after all, a lifelong mariner. The storm was only at Category 3 at the time the ports were closing, a far less dangerous scenario than its arrival. I'd been in other life-threatening situations.

It was my role in life to navigate others to safety in their lives and their businesses. I had no idea that all the predicting, planning, and preparation in the world wouldn't be enough. I had to become my own rescuer.

While you may never have endured a Category 5 hurricane, undoubtedly you have or you will face an extreme Cat 5 event, from other natural disasters to the many storms of life—death, business, relationships, career, money, and anything in between that can render you feeling helpless and uncertain of your survival. Master the Seven Barometers of Resilience introduced in the following chapters to become your own Storm Warrior and prosper in the aftermath of any storm.

"And once the storm is over you won't remember how you made it through, how you managed to survive. You won't even be sure, in fact, whether the storm is really over. But one thing is certain. When you come out of the storm you won't be the same person who walked in. That's what this storm's all about."

—HARUKI MURAKAMI, *KAFKA ON THE SHORE*

PART ONE

THE STORM
WARRIOR

"Only to the extent that we expose ourselves over and over to annihilation can that which is indestructible be found in us."

—PEMA CHODRON

INTRODUCTION
TRAPPED IN A WIND COFFIN

> "And in sleep, pain which cannot forget falls drop by drop upon the heart, until in our own despair, against our will, comes wisdom through the awful grace of God."
>
> —AESCHYLUS

The British Virgin Islands (BVI) rest smack-dab in the middle of Hurricane Alley, the warm-water region from the west coast of North Africa up through the Gulf Coast of the southern United States. Hurricane season is a fact of life for many long-time residents of Hurricane Alley. I loved Tortola, the island where the BVI's capital, Road Town, is located. I was always grateful for my hilltop home there, with its 180-degree view of the islands nestled in the Caribbean Sea and Sir Francis Drake Channel, named after the famous circumnavigator. As a lifelong sailor, I felt connected to the early explorers as I looked out over the same waters that they had sailed to discover the New World.

September 6, 2017, was another day in paradise in the BVI, cloudy but beautiful. It was surreal that a monster storm was coming. Powerful beyond our imagination, it would leave its indelible mark on all of us.

The Saffir–Simpson hurricane wind scale has five categories. The highest on the scale is Category 5, with wind speeds above 156 miles per hour (mph). The other categories are separated by only 20 mph of wind speed, but the difference in power and energy is exponential, the square of the difference. So, a Category 4 is 250 times more powerful than a Category 3, and a

Category 5 is 500 times more powerful than a Category 4. During Hurricane Irma, wind instruments on Tortola were destroyed when the winds exceeded 185 mph, and winds were clocked above 200 mph. That's why Sir Richard Branson, the business mogul who owns two private Caribbean Islands, called Irma a "Category 7 hurricane" after riding out the storm on his Necker island. Comparably, Hurricane Maria that struck Puerto Rico two weeks later and Hurricane Michael the following year were "only" Category 4 hurricanes. (Michael was later reclassified as a Category 5 due to more accurate wind reading information that tipped the scale.)

Hurricanes are a swirling cylindrical column of wind—the first round, or *wall*, comes on from one side. Then there's a strikingly calm period in the eye of the storm before the onslaught of the second wall approaching from the other side. The circumference of Irma measured as large as the state of Ohio, and it was powerful enough to register on the Richter scale.

So, I was alone in my shelter as the winds built

steadily that morning. My windows and sliding glass entry doors were covered and protected except for one set of hurricane-grade windows high above the ground and concealed by dense foliage. I was blissfully ignorant, feeling safe and secure sitting in my "fortress."

That changed by the first wall.

The winds came pounding like a deep, thunderous, angry behemoth screaming sounds I'd never heard before. The monster *tore the roof off* the upstairs. These same panels screwed into my walls had been keeping the storm outside. Water poured through those now-exposed hurricane windows, a thin barricade against the fury of the storm. As water gushed in, I prayed to those windows to hold and keep me safe. It was terrifying. Nothing I'd experienced before prepared me for the **overwhelming force** that descended.

Then came the eye, a respite to assess the situation outside. All the trees were stripped of their leaves and branches. With the roof gone, furniture was flung about, obliterating the upstairs. We were only halfway through, and the landscape was already a wasteland. All my neighbors had also lost most of their roofs by then. Outside, we wandered vacantly, unable to comprehend what had happened. The relentless terror of those first hours left us in shock, fearful about what might come in the next round.

The second onslaught arrived, bringing winds that raged above 200 mph, slamming straight into my sea-facing hilltop home. The storm charged on through the daylight. Because we'd lost power, I was enclosed in darkness, no perception of time or what was happening outside. Inside, only my flashlight's beam gave any reprieve from the artificial night.

My two sliding-glass patio doors were covered by the metal paneling except for a nine-inch opening on each end. Through that small exposure, one of the doors was lifted out of its track by the force, bringing the storm inside. Immediately, the sounds, the water, the debris, the pressure were **unbearably** oppressive. One thing that I didn't understand prior is what the pressure from a major hurricane feels like. If you want to know what it's like, close your mouth, cover your nose, and hold your breath while blowing out for thirty seconds. It feels like being in an airplane ascending to thirty-thousand feet, but the cabin pressure doesn't equalize, your ears never clear and your head feels like it's in a vice grip…for hours.

I checked the other door, now sealed shut by the extreme pressure. I was trapped. The storm poured in through the opening like the tentacles of a monster clawing through my prison bars as I cowered away from its reach. **Shut in**, I had no way to call for help, let alone anyone to call who could come to my rescue. I didn't know how my neighbors were faring. My house had no passing foot traffic on a normal day. It was pitch black. I had no power, no telecoms, **no plan**. Inside my four walls and now porous ceiling, I felt buried alive. I was alone. No one was coming for me. The brutal darkness became more terrifying. I'd spent my life as a professional rescuer, ensuring the safety of other people.

Now *I* needed to be rescued. I could feel the panic rising. I had to do something…**but what could I do?**

So, maybe you haven't been trapped in a wind coffin alone in a record-breaking storm, but have there been times that you felt like you were buried alive by circumstances in your life? Maybe an extreme, seemingly unsolvable financial situation? A business failure? Maybe you've laid awake at night trying to figure out how to pay the rent or make payroll? Suffered divorce, major trauma, illness, the addition or loss of a family member? There are **so many** circumstances that arise that we may be enduring alone, trapped, with no hope of rescue. As an entrepreneur and a human being navigating life, I had this experience countless times before the arrival of Hurricane Irma, but it took this last storm embedding these indelible lessons for me to truly learn how to **survive** and **thrive**.

1

BECOMING YOUR OWN STORM WARRIOR

Harnessing the Power of the Storm

> **"Whatever you are, be a good one."**
> **—WILLIAM MAKEPEACE THACKERAY**

For those almost-twenty-four hours—trapped in my shelter, overwhelmed by my helplessness—I no longer felt like a well-prepared, trained professional rescuer.

My résumé speaks volumes about my penchant for the frontlines—I've been an effective leader, a certified mountain rescuer, professional boat captain, senior executive, business owner, executive coach,

"At a certain moment in [Nietzsche's] life, the idea came to him of what he called 'the love of your fate.' Whatever your fate is…you say, 'This is what I need.' It may look like a wreck, but go at it as though it were an opportunity, a challenge… You will find the strength is there. Any disaster that you can survive is an improvement in your character, your stature, and your life… This is when the spontaneity of your own nature will have a chance to flow. Then, when looking back at your life, you will see that the moments which seemed to be great failures followed by wreckage were the incidents that shaped the life you have now… Nothing can happen to you that is not positive… The crisis throws you back, and when you are required to exhibit strength, it comes."

—JOSEPH CAMPBELL, *REFLECTIONS ON THE ART OF LIVING*

and sought-after advisor to successful entrepreneurs. I've been responsible for ensuring the safety and well-being of countless individuals and enterprises in myriad endeavors all over the world. I worked mostly on my own terms for myself and with partners, committed to flexibility to pursue all my passions. I'd navigated major natural disasters before, including the 1994 Northridge earthquake, where the neighborhood that I worked at was turned into a "war zone," and the 2003 Cedar Fire in San Diego, where we literally had to fight the fire back from our business near the base of Palomar Mountain. I've been first-on-scene a handful of times, voluntarily assisting roadside carnage on remote stretches of highway in the western Rockies during many cross-country ski trips, not to mention my years as an EMT and volunteering on National Ski Patrol, bringing first-aid and safely transporting injured people off mountains.

Before Irma, I wore my feats with pride, bolstered by the illusion that I could bear the weight of any burden. I

before it's too late is a foundational principle of the Storm Warrior. Our Cat 5 events, guided by this principle, teach us how to solve seemingly insurmountable problems. *Merriam-Webster's Dictionary* defines a *cataclysmic event* as one that brings about great change. When these situations are thrust upon us, we can use them for positive change by following the Seven Barometers of Resilience road map introduced in later chapters. With the right attitude, willingness to shed the tendency to go it alone, and harnessing the power of our vulnerability, these upheavals can become life-changing events that propel our lives forward. **Choose** to ask for support where we need it; offer our skills, experience, and expertise to serve wherever we're called; and become a leader in any situation. That is how we become a Storm Warrior.

Harnessing the cataclysmic power of the storms—whether the winds are blowing away your financial security, your company, your home, or life as you know it—is the mission of the Storm Warrior. **Any catastrophic**

situation in life or business can become a vehicle for fulfilling great purpose. Start immediately to use the tools offered here to become your own Storm Warrior. Taking one step at a time will help end any urge to isolate yourself and will turn your vulnerability into your superpower.

ACTION STEPS

▸ Identify situations from your past where you chose to go it alone and prolonged or worsened your situation. Put yourself in the shoes of a rescuer. Who did you burden by your choice, and what could you have done differently to get the support you needed?

▸ Create a list of your most trusted friends, family, or advisors. Choose at least one and let them know that you would like to count on them in the next Category 5 situation you face. Offer to be that person for them.

THIS IS NOT
A DRILL

Living through the Darkest Hours

> "You have power over your mind—not outside
> events. Realize this and you will find strength."
> —MARCUS AURELIUS

In the darkness, trapped behind my barricade with the storm screaming inside, I had no idea how to change my current situation. I knew no one would be coming. It could be days or weeks before anyone might notice if I didn't reappear.

If access to people and all the modern-day tools

were taken away from you—telecommunications, internet access, your community—**how would you approach a problem?** Alone and off the grid, the only tools I had were a pen and paper. A tiny voice in my head said, *Use this experience, learn from it, start writing while you can still remember everything that is happening.* It was the only thing I could control, an action I could take. Writing was something to do while I looked for inspiration to get out of my situation. Writing kept my mind focused, cognitive, and engaging the prefrontal cortex—the problem-solving section of my brain—so the emotional despair couldn't take over. **No matter what you are going through**, you have the power to write down your thoughts if only to activate that analytical part of your brain that solves problem. Develop a practice of writing when something needs to be sorted out; it could even be as simple as making lists. Spending those hours writing is how I began to **learn** from the storm.

Reports from war-torn regions describe refugees becoming immobilized, incapable of cognitive action, sitting in the rubble of what was once their neighbor-hoods, waiting for help to come. We saw this response post-Irma on Tortola. Engaging our cognitive abilities gives us focus, something to do, and small steps to achieve; this even works in the middle of a Category 5 hurricane. Through the hours until daybreak, writing kept my mind attentive and functioning, even when I didn't know how to get out of my situation. In any Cat 5 situation, no matter what or how severe the challenges bearing down on us are, there is always some activity we can do to keep the mind functioning. I was imprisoned for nearly twenty-four hours, and writing moved me beyond my emotions…**activating my ability to reason**.

Breathing deeply to keep the panic at bay, I wrote down everything that I had done to prepare, including everything I'd done right as well as all the mistakes I'd made. I remembered how a friend of mine had men-tioned the night before that she was going to fill her bathtub with water. I had gone to bed that night, and, just as I was starting to unwind, I realized that I hadn't yet filled my tub. I was so glad that I remembered in time because having that tub full of water, and the ability to replenish it in the weeks to come, was a saving grace throughout the remaining months that I had no running water. Working through the lessons learned in real time while waiting out a Cat 5 situation implants them more firmly for the next storm.

I also journaled about what I was feeling and thinking:

Irma took advantage of the vulnerability and literally bent herself into my doors through the cracks. The only thing holding that door in place is the metal walls meant to protect them. Nothing shattered, but it's just sitting there, and all I can do is hope that it stays where it is...

I finished my flood control job but am being defeated by the leaky ceiling above me. With no roof protection and the upstairs flooded, the risk of my ceiling collapsing grows...

Next prayer is that my ceiling stays intact.

Meanwhile, it looks like death outside.

And naturally there's no more internet, so I have no news yet how anyone else is faring.

Water, power, shelter...who would take these for granted? Never me...

As you can see, writing about anything can serve in the middle of a Category 5. It doesn't have to be detailed or profound. Just getting the words out of your head and onto paper—or a screen if you have one—reduces the power of the fear and uncertainty.

Around first light, I discovered a window where the wind had stripped away a corner of the metal panel from the wall outside. A sliver of light shone through like a beacon of hope. I raised the window to allow air in and my voice to be heard if anyone happened to pass by. Eventually I saw someone out there and started screaming for help. The woman managed to gather together three strong men who spent thirty minutes working on freeing me before they could finally manage to get enough leverage to access the heavy glass door from behind the panels and lift it out of its frame to release me from my storm prison.

Stepping out into the sunlight to a post-apocalyptic landscape brought only momentary comfort. The lush green island was now barren and brown as far as I could see. Our road had been partially washed out in the previous month's flooding. It was uncertain if the road, now littered with fallen trees and downed power lines, could bear the weight of vehicles. I was on my own, surrounded only by unfamiliar neighbors—fellow storm refugees without adequate shelter, electricity, running water, or telecoms.

Despair became a constant menace. I had no idea who survived and no way of reaching my friends, local or abroad. In the aftermath, moving from storm-captive to refugee, I had to take responsibility for my survival. Writing during the storm had conditioned my mind to focus and function. I would have to step outside my comfort zone and make new choices to get through the days, weeks, and months ahead.

ACTION STEPS

▸ Develop the habit of writing down your thoughts, wins, and mistakes from any situation that you are facing. Use lists to keep the task simple, manageable, and impactful.

▸ Create a checklist of things, people, and steps you need to consider or prepare for before any storm. Don't forget to keep a pad of paper and a pen nearby just in case!

THE CATASTROPHE AFTER THE CATASTROPHE

Survival and Service

> "The world breaks everyone and afterward many are strong at the broken places."
>
> —ERNEST HEMINGWAY, *A FAREWELL TO ARMS*

Over the next days and weeks, the most adverse survival situation of my life turned into one of the most thriving. Engaging in the activities that I used to first stay alive, then to avoid isolating myself by helping others, brought the Seven Barometers of Resilience to the forefront, which enabled me to become my own Storm Warrior.

that they were safe, plan exit strategies, and get news. So, my connection and service to my new community started with my phone. I had no idea until I gave it a try that I had one of only a couple of working cell phones on the island for weeks. Remember, following any Cat 5 event, stay open and try everything you can think of. Brainstorming with others can yield unexpected resources. **You never know what your undiscovered superpower might be until you listen to everyone and try everything!**

Eventually, I gave my time, energy, and expertise to help with salvage efforts, assisted the UK defense ministry, and coordinated volunteers for an offshore aid organization. Local friends who were off-island during hurricane season began referring media to me once they saw that I could get news out, enabling me to give firsthand reports of conditions on the ground to international news, print, television, and radio out-lets. I shared my impressions to our 35,000-strong BVI Abroad community on Facebook and elsewhere over the following weeks. It was like a pressure release valve for my soul. Before the storm, I couldn't have predicted how to serve my community in the situation. None of those roles were planned or would have occurred to me on my own. They came to me because I stayed in communication. **Stay open, willing, available, and in communication with your community in the post–Category 5 storm. Finding ways to serve and assist others can be a lifesaver.**

Throughout the post–Category 5 catastrophe, I did whatever I could to stay in motion. My activities kept me focused, gave me purpose, and supported my survival. Writing kept me from despair when I was trapped during the storm, and it became the thread that grounded me with a purpose in the aftermath, taking the experience outside of myself. Activity is one of the primary ways to "exercise" the prefrontal cortex so you can eventually solve a seemingly insurmountable problem. Take on whatever tasks emerge to stay in motion. Even the smallest assignments can make all the difference to your survival, so you're not left sitting amidst the rubble waiting for help that might not be coming.

ACTION STEPS

- ▶ Talk to others you know who have endured a comparable Cat 5 situation to find out what worked for them or what they needed but didn't get.

- ▶ Don't be afraid to try everything and speak with everyone. Stay alert to potential solutions you might not be thinking of. Research local community service organizations that you can join or volunteer with—the Red Cross or Rotary International are great places to start.

PART TWO

OUT OF THE RUBBLE

From Resilience into Leadership

"The oak fought the wind and was broken,
the willow bent when it must and survived."

—ROBERT JORDAN, *THE FIRES OF HEAVEN*

4

THE SEVEN BAROMETERS OF RESILIENCE

> **"You may have to fight a battle more than once to win it."**
> —MARGARET THATCHER

The Seven Barometers of Resilience are leadership strategies that got me through the aftermath of Hurricane Irma, enabling me to cope with the trauma, manage the interminable isolation, and make myself useful in my community. Using these Category 5 leadership strategies, I found purpose and a direction to get from surviving to thriving. I don't know how else I could have stayed motivated and kept going. These are the same strategies that I've used to get through other Cat 5 situations and to help clients navigate their own storms. I just hadn't articulated them until I had to confront such an extreme and prolonged life-threatening situation.

First, I had to acknowledge—then abandon—my tendency to withdraw when I was struggling and ask for what I needed, especially as we prepared for more hurricanes, including the Category 5 Hurricane Maria two weeks later. Using these strategies can enable anyone weathering a Cat 5 event to become their own Storm Warrior, create community, and thrive in the aftermath.

You may not think of yourself as a leader if you don't run a business or lead a team, but we are all leaders in multiple settings—in parenting, partnering, social circles, and volunteering, among others. You don't need a formal role or a team to be a leader. I didn't have either on Tortola. I was a resident survivor and refugee.

Leadership refers to how we all manage and conduct ourselves in every situation. With the right tools, we can learn, survive, and flourish in the aftermath of our Category 5 storms.

Let's explore how.

DISCOVER HOW TO CREATE YOUR FLOAT PLAN

> "Any road will get you there if you don't know where you're going."
>
> —LEWIS CARROLL, *ALICE'S ADVENTURES IN WONDERLAND*

A float plan is a tool used by mariners to encapsulate all the details of a voyage—including departure, anticipated conditions, route, destination, timing, equipment, propulsion, and crew—to share with those who are stakeholders in your survival. A float plan reduces the chance of getting caught in any storm with no hope of rescue.

Barometer #1: A float plan can mean the difference between rescue and death to a sailor. Without one, who will come for you in the event of a disaster? How will they know where and when to start looking for you? Create a float plan for success or to hedge against failure. For entrepreneurs, the float plan is like a one-page strategic business plan. I know that for some of us, we hear the phrase *business plan* and our eyes glaze over. We wonder *What would it cost to have someone else create the plan?* and *Is it really necessary?* If you are thinking about an expansion or see a Category 5 event on the horizon, then it sure is. But if you approach the task like a float plan, it isn't as monumental and could be the difference between success and getting "lost at sea" with no chance of rescue...

A float plan contains all of the relevant details related to your journey, so anyone looking at it would know where you are, where you want to go, who's with you, what tools you have or need to get there, a timeline, a communication plan, and a plan for contingencies. It is a cornerstone for my strategic work with small business owners who want to scale any business. Without a float plan, you can wind up like Alice, wandering down the rabbit hole. I'd rather see you get where *you* choose to go!

You can use the float plan to execute your goals and determine how you will get there, so the significant people in your life know where *there* is. Create SMART goals—goals that are Specific, Measurable, Aligned, Realistic, and Time-based—then use your personal float plan to put your SMART goals into action, including outlining the tactics and resources you need along the way as well as any obstacles you could encounter. Using SMART goal–setting with a float plan has helped me effectively achieve some ambitious goals. **Scientific evidence shows that physically handwriting your goals can yield results, because the act of writing connects the brain to the goal**.

Creating a float plan requires you to be aware of and develop a strategy for handling obstacles. Imagine depending on electronic equipment to navigate when suddenly you have no power? What if your food supply required cooking equipment that was no longer functional? Or your water could only be processed by an electronically operated machine? In this technology-mad culture, how far would any of us get without the internet or our smart phones?

What contingency and other plans have you made for your business in the event of a systems failure, and, if you have them, are you keeping them current? Have you shared them with your team? In one of my start-ups, we created a well-developed business plan prior to launch. As the business grew exponentially, we got so busy juggling to keep up, we stopped tracking our results against our projections. **The business plan gathered dust. Don't let that happen to you!**

What if your CFO disappeared or your mate became incapacitated one day without warning? Would you have access to the financial records of the business or the household? Losing a key employee, customer, vendor, or a partner without a plan is a Cat 5 event that can happen to anyone. Is your business protected from such a loss? Would you be able to manage your personal finances without your partner? In one of my businesses, we had to endure the loss of the location where the business had successfully operated for years. Talk about a Cat 5 situation!

Whatever the unique risks in your business—limited client-base, well-financed competition, advancing technology threatening obsolescence, overdependence on a key individual or company—a float plan can help you track the potential risk.

Identify where the enterprise is heading and the necessary tools and equipment that will be needed to reach its destination. Everyone on board needs to know who is on the team and what responsibilities each member has in the mission. Consider the contingencies and have a plan for managing these to safeguard success. The team's enrollment in the mission is critical, so identify what the measuring benchmark is—client acquisition, revenue, profit, product, or service expansion. In my work with entrepreneurs, I've seen smart, successful people launch new products or services without a plan, just *going with their gut*. That might work out fine with some luck, *and* if they never encounter a Cat 5 situation… Inevitably, though, all business owners confront these challenges.

If certain benchmarks in the float plan aren't met, the crew can be prepared, as can your onshore support. "Onshore support" are the people who will come for you in a Category 5 storm (family, friends, investors, partners, vendors, customers). Create your float plan to **ensure a chance of rescue**. Your competency and preparedness will inspire your team to be responsible to what, where, how, and when you'll all get where you're going, reducing the upheaval of the unexpected and enabling you to weather the Cat 5 events we all encounter along the way.

ACTION STEPS

▸ Make a commitment to your team to identify the single skill that would make the biggest impact on the performance of each member in their role:

 ✦ Explore opportunities to provide that skill, allocating an appropriate percentage of your budget on personal/professional development.

 ✦ Try your hand at engaging with that skill set to have a much more intimate view of how to do it, looking objectively at the process to find ways for improvement through additional skills development.

▸ Make an investment in a well-aimed, laser-focused training of specific skills and attitude for the team.

HARNESS THE POWER OF
THE CATEGORY 5 STORM

"Your visions will become clear only when
you can look into your own heart. Who looks
outside, dreams; who looks inside, awakes."

—CARL JUNG

We have an expression in sailing: "Keep one hand on
the boat." Following this guideline ensures that you
have a steadying grip on a constantly shifting, uncertain situation as you move forward on your course.

Barometer #2: "Keep one hand on the boat" is

the rule to move around on a vessel underway. It's a reminder to always be aware of who and where you are, keeping steady and monitoring changing conditions. As the leader, you set the rules and lead by example, making sure your crew stays safe for the duration of any passage. One example of failed leadership occurred during an ocean crossing while a crew was delivering a racing yacht from Tahiti to Los Angeles. The captain— the most experienced crewmember on board—had a habit of going out onto the bow of the boat without being tethered to it. Finally, one of the crew, fearful that the captain was unnecessarily endangering his life (which would, in turn, imperil crew lives) asked him to stop. It is the leader's job to be personally aware of their own conduct and how it might impact others; the example they set; their own needs, resources, and strengths, as well as those of the team; and to conduct themselves in the manner they expect from others. I overlooked this responsibility in the first storm.

Conditions in life and business are just as fluid.

Market forces, technology advances, evolving competition, and people require us to keep "one hand on the boat" at all times. I always tell my technology start-up clients they should anticipate that the lifespan of their new tech idea may be about six months from launch, after which time it could become obsolete or be improved by a bigger and better-financed competitor, so they needed to plan for longevity, not just to go to market.

Staying aware of ourselves and our situations allows us to create forward momentum and growth by managing our needs and maintaining respect for ourselves and our significant others. In the pressure of the Category 5 storm, these practices can be abandoned if we aren't cognizant of others weathering their own storms. Know where you are at any given moment, what your needs and capacity are, and how to stay tethered to the mission. Knowing that your team is also committed to staying on board and setting clear expectations makes prospering possible. When you are all aware of

what the situation requires, with a steady grip through-out the Cat 5, you can take one step at a time without getting thrown overboard.

Self- and situational-awareness are the most crit-ical leadership skills we can develop to navigate a Category 5 situation.

Humans are conditioned by external circumstances; we respond to triggers. Self-awareness helps us differ-entiate when we're responding to the triggering event and when we're responding to a narrative about the trigger. Most of our responses are autonomic—reflexes that come from the way we've been conditioned by our past experiences. Our tendency is to respond to stimuli and interpret them through the lens of this condition-ing, the story we tell ourselves about it. This relates to the idea of *self-concept*. The self-concept is made up of self-image, self-ideal, and self-esteem. We all have a self-concept that dictates how our lives turn out, usu-ally established from early childhood, based on how we were loved, accepted, criticized, or rejected when we were young. Your self-concept controls how self-aware you are and your responses in a Cat 5 event. In extreme situations, take a moment to identify what are the **actual** sensory components, what is **really** going on independent of the narrative. This allows us to become more self-aware, differentiating whether we are responding to the Cat 5 situation or to the story in our head about the situation.

Bolster situational awareness by maintaining a thirty-thousand-foot view of what you're facing to make decisions from there, rather than fleeing on the ground from a very uncomfortable situation. With the big picture in mind, identify your abilities, limitations, and resources, then learn from the experience as you go forward in the aftermath. **In my own Category 5 storm, by staying attentive, I could serve my community every day while also taking care of my own needs.**

Do a deep clarity dive to build an actionable, steadying road map for yourself or for your business, starting wherever you are right now. This tool will support you through a Cat 5 event. Identify what is expected of you as a leader, who you are meant to serve, how you solve the problem they want you to solve for them, and where you want to go in the short-, medium-, and long-term. Taking these steps prior to the storm will help you keep one hand on the boat!

ACTION STEPS

▶ Develop the skill of self-awareness; find ways to measure and heighten it and to develop your intrapersonal skills as a leader.

▶ Reach out to those you know, love, and trust to give you their perceptions of you under normal circumstances, under moderately stressful circumstances, and under extremely stressful circumstances. Then compare this feedback with your self-perception to see how consistent they are.

7

MANAGE THE CATASTROPHE AFTER THE CATASTROPHE

> "'I think,' said Christopher Robin, 'that we ought to eat all our provisions now, so that we shan't have so much to carry.'"
>
> —A. A. MILNE

When setting sail offshore, we apply expedition rules to ensure we have everything that we can plan for and we have backups for the situations we can't predict.

Barometer #3: Expedition planning and preparation allow you to maintain situational readiness. Anyone

I was managing cash flow for one of my companies, I always made sure that I paid vendors in a timely manner when times were flush to build up a reputation as a good payer. That way, if we ever needed some leeway, vendors were happy to advance credit or extend terms.

In another one of my start-ups, we experienced rapid growth, going from a team of 3 to a team of 160 within just a few months. In order to keep control, we rapidly implemented operational, financial, and HR systems to ensure the company could handle the growth and stay legally compliant. This structure gave the team a solid understanding of what was expected and how we operated, even as we invented it along the way. These operational systems and department guidelines meant that the team always knew what was expected of them. Then we could expand on these as we grew and gained intel.

Expedition rules apply even if you haven't done any preparation ahead of time. Post-Irma, we had to go weeks without running water in our community. A marina assuaged the situation by leading pipes from its reverse-osmosis plant out to the roadway, providing free potable water to passersby, something that had never been done before. With transportation, I could take immediate advantage of this resource. Keep a watch for resources and opportunities that may be available to you to help you navigate your Category 5 storm; engage and rally your team to fill the needs called for by the situation, inspiring everyone (including yourself) to move forward purposefully.

Know how to work within a team, set expectations, and let everyone take responsibility for survival so that everyone knows their responsibilities, counts on the others, and doesn't have to pick up slack—**these rules will safeguard your survival,** whether you are climbing a glacier, sailing offshore, growing a business, or taking a family vacation!

ACTION STEPS

► Within the group, identify and document the qualities and characteristics that make a positive learning environment for the team that everyone commits to. Create internal accountability using that document to maintain the positive environment.

► Identify some tools that you can implement within your organization to keep your team calm and for conflict resolution. Create safe *containers* for bringing up conflict and tensions early, before they become corrosive for your organization.

DEVELOP A CATEGORY 5 LEADERSHIP STYLE

"Anyone can hold the helm when the sea is calm."

—PUBLILIUS SYRUS

When disaster strikes, you need to find a role that serves yourself, your team, your family members, and your community.

Barometer #4: In a Category 5 situation, your ability to be successful and contribute in the aftermath of the event will depend on having and using the vision to assume a leadership role. Imagine setting out to prepare a dish that you have never prepared before, maybe something you've seen in a magazine or on a cooking show. What is the first thing that you do? You visualize the finished dish. There is nothing more important in culinary artistry (or artistry in any form) than to have a really clear vision in your mind of your outcome. Then you can work backward, get your timing right, and prepare your ingredients properly to get to that goal. In setting out on any journey, it can be as simple as plotting a course to a destination from where you are; taking a bearing; calculating how many days it will take to get there; being able to monitor supplies, progress, and conditions; and comparing your *dead reckoning* (the theoretical course plot) to what is actually happening in ever-changing conditions.

If you can see the possibilities in your situation, you can step up to move the community forward as a leader and assume one of four leadership roles that you can shoulder in the Category 5 landscape. The National Outdoor Leadership School (NOLS) outlines the four styles for expedition leadership as follows: designated leader, peer leader, self-leader, active followership.

The **designated leader** is an appointed role that is evident to everyone and carries certain authority. Irma was unsparing in her destruction—occupation, wealth, success, education, title—none of these could stave off the onslaught. Consequently, we could not count on our government officials, the designated leaders in our community. So, the community had to be served by other kinds of leaders.

Peer leadership involves playing your part on the team to work together toward common goals. This form of leadership is not designated. It is important that each member of the team recognizes what needs to be done and takes the initiative to go do it. Peer leadership is empowering to the team. Post-Irma, off-shore and local organizations and individuals banded together to assist the recovery—including facilitating evacuations and the inflow of food, water, medical supplies, and personnel. Hurricane Maria forced the withdrawal of support from our Puerto Rican neighbors. With local supplies mostly diminished or inaccessible and other resources from abroad unreachable to our remote island, the situation was dire. Much could be accomplished with peer leadership engaged in the recovery.

Self-leadership involves building a culture where everyone takes care of themselves to the best of their ability, showing personal initiative and character. This is the single most important leadership role. Self-leadership will inspire peer leadership, and through that can come a much more evolved and mature active followership.

Active followership is recognizing the importance of being a really engaged supporter to that designated leadership role, participating in the group decision-making process by giving input and seeking clarity. This is another hugely valuable leadership role.

In the post–Category 5 catastrophe, you can choose any combination of these roles, even if you weren't a designated leader with an official title previously. **Leader-survivors look for what is needed in the community**, choose a role that they are well-suited for and that best enables them to contribute to the improvement of the situation, the team, the business, their own lives, and that of their families, without waiting for an official assignment—that is how *I* found my purpose in the Category 5 aftermath.

In a Cat 5 situation, good, visionary, willing crew members are essential to the recovery. Following the disaster, people are focused on their own needs and recovery and may not be capable of asking for help. A leader in the aftermath looks at what's needed and steps forward without stepping on toes. Anyone can come forward—whether it is to volunteer or take on a designated role. In one start-up, I used to call myself COO, General Counsel, and Chief Toilet-Paper-Roll-Changer. You must be willing to do what it takes to flourish. **It doesn't matter who you were before; it's about who you become in the aftermath.**

Even if you are not comfortable taking a more forward leadership role, active followership is always an option. Excellent active followership skills are how we run a successful yacht racing crew. Each member knows and executes their own jobs well but also stays aware of and helps manage any situation that arises, contributing key intel and action to keep the team on course to reach the finish line. The most successful teams are those where everyone knows that they can count on all the other members of the team in the event of an emergency. Use your vision to see what needs to be accomplished, then take any kind of action to motivate others around you, give you purpose in the aftermath of the storm, and keep you from becoming immobilized following a Cat 5 event.

ACTION STEPS

▸ Examine how your vision is articulated within your organization or community, how the members interpret it, and how well their interpretation aligns to your vision as a leader.

▸ Find ways within the culture to bring greater alignment to your vision as a leader. Relate the understanding expressed by your team to your core ideology and how one supports the other.

9

BUILD YOUR TRIBE TO WEATHER ANY STORM

"You gain strength, courage, and confidence by every experience in which you really stop to look fear in the face. You must do the thing you think you cannot do."
—ELEANOR ROOSEVELT

In a Category 5 storm, you may not have access to friends and family or those who you would count on in ordinary circumstances. Be willing to get out of your comfort zone and build community so you don't go it alone, and you can thrive in the aftermath.

Barometer #5: As I shared already, I had to discover the hard way the consequences of *going it alone*. I know now that it was mindless, habitual behavior. You may be someone who resorts to similar behavior in your own storms, not seeing that there are steps you can take to avoid winding up alone.

About a month after the first storm, a restaurant had reopened on the island. A few of us gathered for dinner among the ruins of what had once been a favorite place. We each shared our stories of how we weathered the storm, what we did to prepare, what happened to us in those hours and days immediately following. We went around the table one-by-one as everyone listened intently. When at last it was my turn, I shared my story. When I got to the end, I said, "And I was alone." Everyone at the table gasped! It was the first time that I saw myself through the lens of other survivors, and I realized in that instant that I didn't know anyone else who had endured the storm *alone*.

In that moment, I had a glimpse of how much more I compounded my own situation and the ensuing trauma by not asking for help or seeking refuge with people I knew. It didn't occur to me to ask any of my friends scattered around the island if I could stay with them. Even during the storm's destruction after the first wall, I chose solitude instead of strangers! How many situations in my past did I make worse because I'd made that mistake? Who else had I burdened by my own mindlessness?

Maybe you're thinking, *That's not me. I don't isolate myself from people.* Ask yourself, when you have a heavy burden to bear or feel ashamed, humiliated, or uncomfortable, are there people in your life to share your experience with, or do you avoid talking about it with anyone? Is there anything significant going on in your life now that you would rather no one know about? And if so, why? As a serial entrepreneur and risk-taker, there have been times when I have endured extremely difficult financial distress that I never wanted to share. I would avoid socializing. I would tell myself it was out of necessity, but really it was because I didn't want anyone to know what was really going on.

The solitary lifestyle I was living up until Irma was easy to lean into, because it is an accepted state in our culture—we learn at an early age that self-sufficiency is rewarded and that we should be independent problem-solvers. The world encourages this by isolating us in our cars, our ear buds, and our social media platforms. Such behavior leads to further separation, often under the illusion of inclusion. Like many of you, I was active on social media, connected to people all over the world. I was involved in outdoor activities— like my weekly hiking group and team sports like yacht-racing—that involved communities of people. I never thought of myself as isolated. I was alone only when I chose to be, but social activities and online connections alone cannot make up a real community. Real community is having people who will come for us in a storm. We create that by offering to be that person for others first.

How did I end up alone in the aftermath of the storm? Had I mistaken my hundreds of Facebook friends and thousands of social media followers for community?

Professionally I was well-paid for my good advice and knowledge. Yet, secretly, I held an unspoken belief that I had to "do it on my own" or else people might find out that I was, at times, fearful and uncertain. When I went after my captain's license, I could have used guidance to navigate the arduous application process. Instead of asking a dear friend who was a very experienced captain, I struggled to get it done by myself. I was surprised talking about it with him later that he thought I *wanted* to do it on my own, like I wanted to prove something. I hadn't realized then that I'd made it seem like I didn't want help. How many times had my own actions kept people from offering help?

Subconsciously, I believed that if I shared my doubts about handling whatever situation was in front of me, it would make me seem less capable in others' eyes. Yet the consequent isolation that comes from such fallacious thinking is a direct contributor to a worldwide epidemic of depression, anxiety, and suicide in every age group. According to the 2018 landmark study by Cigna in partnership with Ipsos, nearly 40 percent of our population has **no one to talk to**!

In each storm that I weathered alone, it wasn't because I didn't want or have people around me, but because I was afraid to let people know when times were tough or when I needed support. I would rather pretend that everything was fine or simply disappear until it was. This was how I dealt with financial difficulties, business challenges or failures, the collapse of intimate relationships, and a divorce.

Can you relate?

Maybe you've experienced financial challenges, had to curtail social activities, then avoided contact with even trustworthy friends to whom you might confide. Maybe you were like me, and you've had your heartbroken and pretended to your friends that everything was fine. Maybe, like me, you found yourself in conflict with business partners and were forced out of a business that you helped start and, other than your legal representatives, you didn't share with anyone the extreme difficulties and emotional upheaval that you experienced in the process.

If you never encountered any of those situations, maybe you have experienced some upheaval, some distress that might be categorized as Category 5—extreme beyond your ability to manage on your own, like a major illness, trauma, or loss of a family member. You may have weathered these experiences on your own, without confiding in anyone, as many people do. But the consequences of going it alone can be severe, as I discovered. Each time I chose to endure one of these life or business events alone, my outer shell got tougher to penetrate, reinforcing my tendency to isolate myself, because I never developed the tools to communicate my vulnerability when I was in trouble. I was not yet a Storm Warrior. I thought if I handled these situations on my own, that meant that I was strong, in control, and capable of taking care of others. **But who would rescue the rescuer?**

I have never been someone who didn't have friends. I cultivate people around me that I genuinely love. If you knew me personally, you might think that I had many people around me to confide in. But for most of my life, I chose isolation rather than confiding in anyone who might discover that I didn't "have it all together." It was my job, after all, to ensure the safety and well-being of others in their endeavors.

Remember that our self-concept is the thermostat for our comfort zone that determines our beliefs, outcomes, successes, and failures. Without conscious intervention, we keep ourselves within 10 percent of the familiar setting that we can tolerate, even when it increases our suffering. The self-concept is triggered in Category 5 storms, and quite often, go-to behaviors won't galvanize us in the aftermath. Before the disaster strikes, expand your tolerance for adversity by expanding your comfort zone. How it is developed is important. Keep enough of a balance in and out of the zone that you're still learning but not so far out of the zone that you are triggering the fight-or-flight mode or can no longer process what is before you. Make sure you're stretching enough that it is stimulating in a way that allows you to feel like you're working hard and you are challenged and enduring something out of the ordinary.

Turning up your capacity to handle adversity allows you to turn challenges into opportunities. Adapt to changed circumstances using humor to create your community out of the strangers around you. Learn what your comfort zone settings are on your personal self-concept thermostat and be prepared to dial it up!

ACTION STEPS

▸ Find ways that you can magnify the comfort zone of you and your team.

▸ Expand your team's comfort zone by building confidence so they can respond effectively in more stressful situations.

  + Use an off-site location that contains elements unrelated to the work that you might normally do.

  + Put yourselves into new situations.

+ Drop your hierarchy and explore the natural leadership abilities of the team outside of their roles. Often that uncertainty will give rise to a new-found capacity.

▸ Try a great metric: do something scary and fun (trapeze outing, mountain climbing, and sailing are a few ideas I've used).

KEEP THE EMERGENCY CHANNEL OPEN

> "The one easy way to become worth 50 percent more than you are now—at least—is to hone your communication skills—both written and verbal."
>
> —WARREN BUFFETT

It is the law of the sea to monitor U.S. Coast Guard Emergency Channel 16.

Barometer #6: In a Category 5 storm, communications are **critical**, as I discovered so painfully when I couldn't communicate during Irma. On the water, we are required to monitor the U.S. Coast Guard's emergency station for all near-coastal communications at sea. The radio is tuned to this channel by default when underway.

I love the protocol of **call and response**. Ever since humans started going to sea, regardless of the culture, when a communication is made, some response is given that acknowledges that that communication was heard, that checks for clarity and demonstrates compliance. In very rudimentary terms, in the modern world, it is an element that is often overlooked in our communications. If we can find ways to bring that back and to create more effective communication, our culture will be positively impacted. Individual performance will improve, engagement will increase, and we'll all feel better about wanting to lead, to work, to grow, and to succeed following any Category 5 situation.

Consider how you will communicate with your local community, your team, or your family and friends before, during, and after an extreme event.

Communicating what you think, feel, and need elicits a response from those in a position to help. I didn't consider how I would let my family and friends know that I was alive or alert anyone if I needed help. I was lucky the woman passing by my window heard me that fateful day. I had not even let those who loved me the most know how to find out if I'd survived!

Before the Category 5 strikes, develop a plan for contingency communications, assign responsibilities for transmitting information, and manage the expectations of the people with a stake in your survival. Figure out how you will get information to and from the disaster zone and monitor conditions inside and outside the affected area. Stay in touch with your local community to keep informed of the constantly changing circumstances and impending events. Remember that truck driving down the waterfront road with the loudspeaker communicating that a hurricane was headed toward us three days after Irma? Don't let that be you, trying to reach people who can't hear you with information that is unreliable and insufficient and instructions they can't do anything about.

The communication piece is the metric of other leadership skills too. How do we take that communication skill into a Category 5 situation that doesn't cause us to regress? I've been on race boats where the skipper yells at the crew during certain situations—a behavior that speaks to a level of incompetence. The stress level is inappropriate in such moderate conditions. The skipper, under stress, erodes confidence, raising questions about his ability to safely lead the vessel. Had he learned and practiced how to more effectively handle the boat in those conditions and had a clearer vision of the steps required, the stress level wouldn't have been so high.

As leaders, we get the most out of people through our mastery of communication styles, skills, and effectiveness. Who you are and how you communicate can create great success, or it can alienate you from your team or community. Know and understand your own

communication style and that of your team members who will step up in the Cat 5 situation. If you can motivate, inspire, praise, and critique them in a way that can be received, it will directly impact how you all come through the storm.

Be an attentive listener too. Acclaimed author Stephen Covey says, "Seek first to understand, then to be understood." Ask a lot of questions, repeat back what you heard, smile, and put people at ease so they

ACTION STEPS

▸ Know your own behavioral style. What is it that drives how you respond to information? Study your responses in different situations—using the right tool can provide incredibly poignant insight as to how you communicate.

▸ Get insight into why you respond the way that you do. Learn the driving forces that build real satisfaction and start to incorporate that in your own communication for yourself and for your team. This is the foremost thing you should do to manage any relationships, situations, or outcomes, and where I always start with new clients.

▶ Explore some communication tools that resonate with you—what are the conflict resolution tools that you can teach your team to use? What are the active listening tools you can use to incorporate into your team meetings? What are the forms and structure you're going to use to give or exchange feedback—both positive and constructive? Create an environment of greater self-management through the development of competence so that the team can become better problem-solvers, answer questions for themselves, and have the support they need to be confident acting in those positions.

11

COMMIT TO
A COURSE

**"Good judgment comes from experience, and
experience comes from bad judgment."**

—RITA MAE BROWN

In a Category 5 storm, good judgment and critical
decision-making skills are necessary; in high-stakes
situations, mistakes can be devastating, so know when
to *reef the main*.

Barometer #7: Developing good judgment is critical, no more so than in a Category 5 situation. On a

sailboat, the sails are the propulsion device to power the boat. When heading into heavy winds, you need to reduce the propulsion to not get overpowered by the conditions. Reducing the amount of sail area through reefing (shortening the size and number of the sails that you are using) reduces power, much like lifting the gas pedal on your car while driving around corners. If you don't reduce speed, you could lose control. Racetracks are lined with rubber to hone this skill. And, just like racing around corners, with experience you improve your timing of when to throttle back.

Knowing when to reef the main is an art form, the mastery of which increases your chance of surviving whatever is coming. A well-known axiom of sailors is that "if you're thinking about reefing, it's already too late!" The only way to develop good instincts about reefing is to experience the consequences of waiting too long. I had to learn from the mistakes that I made in the Cat 5. By honoring our past, we access our ability to develop good judgment. We can also leverage the experience of those around us who've had experiences we've not had and bring that broader scope into developing greater judgment.

Develop good judgment and decision-making skills to handle any storm that comes our way by being willing to make decisions and suffer the consequences. Failure to do so leads to complacency, and the number one law of seamanship is *complacency kills.* This is true in relationships, business, money, career, and life. Managing limited cash flow whether it's in your life or your business is one such example where good judgment must be developed, because the consequences can be severe if you don't. If money is tight, you need to rein in spending, even if your growth plans are decelerated. Otherwise you could end up in crushing debt that you cannot service, or out of business.

In yacht racing, the tactician is responsible for maintaining the "back-of-the-boat" perspective, making the critical decision of when to go left or right. If they make the right choice, the skipper takes the credit, but if they make the wrong choice, they get the blame. We are all tacticians in the volatile conditions in our own lives and businesses. We must absorb all the information available—the position of our company, the competition, market trends, technology advances—and keep our eye on the big picture, knowing that our decisions can have varying degrees of consequences. Be willing to move forward and risk being wrong, then learn from your choices, recognizing that the best you can do is mitigate the risk as you develop good instincts.

Start by first developing a decision-making style with your team. Then practice and create a decision-making plan for execution in a Cat 5 situation. What is your preferred style? Do you rule by directive when you make a decision? Is it going to be consultative? Are you going to seek information from the team before choosing? Have you already chosen, and are you checking in with them or retaining the right to decide after you check in with them? Will you use a consensus style where everyone must agree before you can move forward and you're all going to have to compromise to get there? Or is this going to be a democratic process? If so, are you willing to give up control, give everyone one vote, and relinquish the right to make that decision? Or are you going to delegate to someone else and let them take responsibility for this inquiry?

A race boat is not a democracy. The crew understands that while they may have information to share that will be impactful, they don't have a vote. In an enterprise, such an autocratic style can cause resentment and even a mutiny outside a well-defined organizational structure. It can also mean that you miss critical input.

In choosing a decision-making style, two considerations will influence you:

1. How much time do you have to decide?

2. How important is it for the execution to get the group to buy into this decision?

In a Category 5 situation, the designated leader might not be in the best position to make the decision. There may be others on the team or outside the team who either have better, more informed data, or who may have experienced the same situation in the past who you want to rely on in the Cat 5 event. Be creative in your process, leverage the strength of your group, and stay open to a style that is most likely to yield the best outcome under the circumstances, even if you, the designated leader, aren't the final arbiter.

A client of mine ran his department in such a way that **emboldened** everyone on the team. Each year at bonus time, he let the team know what his budget was for the entire division and invited them to decide how it should be allocated. No one ever complained, and the result was always equitable. Another leadership technique he employed successfully was to give problem-solving responsibility to the person most closely connected to executing the solution. This decision-making style worked well for his team and the feedback from his 360-degree reviews was always positive.

I had a tendency in the past with one start-up company to be more **protective** managing my team through tight cash-flow situations. I wanted to shelter them from feeling insecure about the stability of the business if I shared too much information. I never wanted them to know how precarious our financial situation was, only that they should look for cost savings wherever they could. Perhaps if I'd been a little more forthcoming, I would have had greater enrollment and better relationships at the time. The feedback I got in my reviews was that they understood the pressure that I was under but didn't understand my communication style. I had work to do to win them over. **Choose a decision-making style and communicate it to the team no matter the consequences.** Eventually, you will develop good judgment to thrive in any Category 5 situation.

ACTION STEPS

▸ Actively identify and practice decision-making models for every decision you're making.

▸ Publicly identify the way you're going to make your decisions.

▸ Train the team in the vocabulary and process of each of those decision-making styles so that when you say "I'm going to delegate," they understand what that means. When you say "I have yet to make that decision, but I'm going to use a consensus style," they understand it's an opportunity for them to have input and that you're going to leverage their buy-in.

▶ Explore the experiences of your team that have helped them develop good judgment, including the following:

+ Discover troubles they have encountered that you can draw on when you're in those future situations.

+ Look at the bad outcomes they've experienced— bad outcomes are like the process of making lemonade. It's not one lemon that gives you lemonade; it's a series that's required.

+ Identify small decisions they've made along the way that are now going to inform you to make a better decision next time.

PART THREE

CLEAR SKIES
AND
CALM SEAS

"Efforts and courage are not enough
without purpose and direction."

—JOHN F. KENNEDY

12

HOMECOMING

The Isolation Can Bury You Even in the Land of Plenty

> "Ye cannot live for yourselves; a thousand fibres connect you with your fellow-men."
>
> —HENRY MELVILL, "PARTAKING IN OTHER MEN'S SINS"

I managed to overcome my isolation and get in motion while I was on my island with my fellow survivors to contribute to my community and begin to **thrive**. However, my eventual return to the United States seemed to set me right back into isolation. In a Category 5 storm that we experience with others, we have a shared bond with the survivors as we navigate our recovery. But if we are enduring a Cat 5 on our own, like a divorce, an illness, or the end of a relationship, it can feel more isolating, because no one else is going through the storm with us. Returning to the States, where the devastation of the hurricane was off the radar, left me alone in my recovery. Surviving and thriving in the immediate aftermath with my fellow islanders was only the first step in my personal healing process. I couldn't go back there, and what was in front of me no longer fit.

When an extreme Category 5 event impacts us singularly, like a death or divorce, it can be very difficult to reintegrate with people who are simply going about their lives. If we don't share the circumstances with anyone, the situation gets worse. With so much of our population having no one to talk to, isolation and loneliness are already rampant. The global health crisis of suicide, depression, and anxiety is amplified in the Cat 5 situation.

This tendency toward isolation isn't just a social problem. It can also be an issue in our professional lives. I have sat in the C-suite chair in a number of enterprises, feeling so alone at times, fraught that anyone understood the pressures that my job placed on me—running a team of over a 150 people; managing the tight cash flow of an underfunded, rapidly growing enterprise; dealing with a protracted and costly business litigation; lying awake at night worrying about lease payments, payroll, and debt service—these are just a few of the demands of being a small business owner that can lead to you feeling completely alone.

With the advent of what we now commonly refer to as the *gig economy*, more people are freelancing their services and working alone in their home spaces or alone in common professional workspaces without a team around them. There is no respite at the water cooler to swap stories, exchange ideas, or talk about the latest Netflix release. In fact, the social isolation and consequent loneliness of the solopreneur is so rampant that some experts argue that it is a large contributor to the failure of many these solo entrepreneurial businesses. I've happily worked that way many times in my career. I never stopped to think about what I was giving up or what habits I was developing that would one day leave me trapped alone in a storm shelter.

I also work regularly with senior executives in transition, most of whom have managed large teams in their past jobs. One of the common complaints they have in dealing with their transition is that they miss being around people, being able to exchange ideas. They are unsure how to recover what they've lost in an evolving economic landscape—a long-standing, secure position in a company that values their wisdom, experience, and expertise. The pervading isolation affects those who find themselves downsized in a changing industry while at the height of their value and contribution. Nowhere is this more prevalent than the entertainment industry, where I have worked for twenty-five years. I facilitate monthly roundtable discussions with these executives and encourage participants to meet regularly, share resources, and support each other so they don't isolate. Downsizing, consolidation, and globalization are putting senior leaders into a Category 5 situation looking at a long road ahead to land their next role.

I know that, prior to the hurricanes, I shouldered most of my burdens alone, especially when there was a personal crisis such as a financially challenging time or the heartbreak of a failed relationship.

Gravitating toward bearing our struggles in private is part of our culture. We are prized for our independence, conditioned to believe that showing vulnerability is a sign of weakness. Then we **silo ourselves** into our geography, religion, politics, and economics. Recognizing this common behavior—especially when the Category 5 situation is raging—is a vital step to becoming a Storm Warrior. Heeding the lessons from the storms to find the power in my own vulnerability

while serving my community is how I became my own rescuer. In doing so, I overcame the despair in the aftermath and began to live with more purpose and greater capacity to be of service in the world. **Become a Storm Warrior so you can too.**

ACTION STEPS

▸ Find like-minded, similarly situated people who share your life or business circumstances. Create a master-mind group that meets regularly, keeping the group small enough to manage and set clear guidelines about active, non-judgmental listening.

▸ Reach out to someone who is experiencing their own Category 5 storm and offer to support them. Volunteer with local service organizations that provide natural disaster aid to meet others who are similarly predisposed to serve their communities.

CONCLUSION
RECREATING COMMUNITY WITH PURPOSE

"Start where you are. Use what
you have. Do what you can."

—ARTHUR ASHE

When disaster strikes, people often come together in religious houses and other venues to talk to each other, setting ideology aside. As we discovered on post-Irma Tortola, our common cause of survival creates unlikely bonds among people. From unimaginable tragedy, there is more unity...but then it dissipates. In the aftermath of every Category 5 storm, we briefly taste what community could be, until we return to homeostasis—**seclusion.**

We can measure this disconnectedness in and out of crisis by what I've coined the **isolation index**. Our level of separation can be tracked on a scale through inquiry and self-assessment, weighing such indicative factors as frequency of communication with others, appetite for social activity, and hair-trigger emotional responses. Isolation can also be measured collectively within our social circles as we wall ourselves in among shared beliefs, creating an insurmountable chasm of separation. Irma catapulted me and my fellow islanders to a 9.5 out of 10. When it came down to my survival, I had no choice but to climb out of the rubble to create connection. Your survival, or at least your ability to move forward, may depend on knowing where you fall on the scale.

Measure your own isolation index by asking yourself these three questions and rating your response on a scale of 1–10 of least likely to more likely:

1. Am I quicker to get angry/sad/depressed/silent following a crisis?

2. Do I take myself out of communication when hit by a devastating blow to my life, business, monies, relationships, or health?

3. Do I turn down invitations from loved ones and friends for no reason or simply to avoid engaging with others?

Where are you on the isolation index today, individually, and communally?

The strategies that I used to survive and prosper on Tortola and to become my own Storm Warrior in the

aftermath of the catastrophe can be useful to anyone weathering their own Category 5 storms.

After enduring a Cat 5 event, create a new float plan, redefine your vision, and commit to deepening your relationships with people through more vulnerable connections. Use the Category 5 leadership strategies we've discussed here to build the framework for the next phase of your life or business. Become more mindful about your decisions and their impact so you don't go home alone to weather a storm. Build a community around you of those who know the truth about what you have been through, your struggles and your triumphs. Share your story to bring comfort to someone and help them feel a little less alone in the face of their own Category 5 storms.

It takes time to integrate your Cat 5 experiences. Once I let my friends and colleagues know what was going on, I could count on their generosity to help me begin the true healing process. Figure out what you need to start your cathartic process of healing in the aftermath of a Category 5 event.

When you are confronted with an extreme situation, be willing to tell at least one trusted person, someone who can listen without judgment and who could perhaps share their own Cat 5 experiences. Each time you do so is a step closer to healing and recovery, as you gain more clarity about what you learned both from the most recent storm and the storms you've weathered throughout your life. Following these Cat 5 experiences, I chose to share my learning with others, hoping it would free them to tell their own Category 5 stories to keep *anyone* from enduring these storms alone without the tools to prosper.

Become your own Storm Warrior. With the power of authentic vulnerability, you will bring in more support because others will know what is really going on and that you may not have it all together. People generally want to be helpful. You will build deeper, more trusting relationships, including new business and friendships that are richer, more supportive, deeper, and more accepting. The depth of your work can expand in a more authentic way. This is the gift of the Category 5 storm, the power that you can harness by becoming a true Storm Warrior. You are not alone. None of us should ever be, if only we can channel our vulnerability to flourish in the aftermath of our Category 5 storms.

These storm experiences were my greatest teachers, enabling me to create a more purposeful life—one with more meaning and clarity. I'd been on this journey of self-discovery and problem-solving throughout my life. Until this last storm, I couldn't see how my choices were keeping me isolated from a real community—or the burden I was putting on others by keeping them at a distance—until it was nearly too late. Over time and with perspective, I could get to work helping others discover how to become their own Storm Warrior.

In your own Category 5 storms, there are many things that you can do, even as the storm is still raging, to ensure your survival and to come through to thrive:

- Use your ability to write in order to learn from your experiences and to prevent the challenges from compromising your ability to solve problems and take over your sense of who you are.

- If you find yourself isolating, create a lifeline to bridge the divide by reaching out to those enduring the same impact or their own version of a Category 5 storm.

- Your social media connections may not be reachable or able to help you, so become adept at building local community under any circumstance, including among strangers. Otherwise, who will come for you in a storm?

- Although it is seemingly impossible at times, we can always find ways to be of service. Start locally, assist in any capacity to get the help you need in the aftermath of a Category 5 storm.

- We can endure any storm if we don't go it alone. Practice asking for help. Being the most vulnerable is the true challenge of the Cat 5 situation.

When we're called forth to assist others, we become our own Storm Warrior, finding a port in and after every storm through community.

Finally, we know there's always going to be another Category 5 storm, whether the winds are blowing away your roof, your relationship, your business, or your life. These storms can create great change and forward movement in the world—turning a catastrophe into a cataclysm for change. Great change can lead us to great purpose. Each of us gets to choose if we are the storm's victim or we are empowered by the storm.

Every day since that first new dawn when I was rescued from my shelter prison, I have endeavored to be of the highest service, to listen to my heart's true desire, and to live authentically. This is the same journey we are all on. You can use these Cat 5 events to become a Storm Warrior so you never have to endure another storm alone. You can survive and thrive in any Category 5 storm to reach clear skies and calm seas by becoming a Storm Warrior.

ACKNOWLEDGMENTS

It isn't often that one can use the expression "you're a lifesaver" and have it mean something quite literal. I have been blessed (and cursed?!) with that opportunity, and for those of you I am fortunate to be able to acknowledge below, and countless others, you are undoubtedly the reason that I am still here. You have given me shelter, and at times held up a mirror to teach me the lessons I needed to weather this and every other storm in my life: Divanna Vadree, Darlene Winter,

Mathew, Edith and John Perakis, Sanjay Soni, Peter Kadlubski, Wayne Crawford, Kevin Goetz, Paula Shaw.

This book was conceived the moment I realized that I was trapped in my wind coffin. And, even as I had no idea what it would take to turn it into something I could share with the world, I knew that I would not be able to figure it out alone. Gratefully, I didn't have to. I was immediately embraced by an extraordinary community of people who saw something in my story and helped me make sense of the fact that I was still alive to tell it—Hans Trupp, Adam Farfan, Ken Rutkowski, Isaac Mizrahi, Michael Breus, Greg Small, Heidi Hubbeling-Leach, Geoffrey Berwind, Steve Harrison, Debra Englander, Martha Bullen, Patsy Cisneros, Raia King, Tamra Nashman, Lizet Zayas, Josh Tapp, Ryan Crownholm, John P. Morgan, Mark Goulston, Adrian Ulsh, Karl Bryan, George Kansas, Tracey Trottenberg— you spent immeasurable hours giving me so much support to help me turn this most terrifying event of my life into something that others might be able to see themselves in and benefit from. But most importantly, you showed me that I wouldn't have to weather the aftermath of any storm alone!

And there are those who rescued me "from the rubble," including Jeffrey Skelton and the Skelton family, Charlotte Matthews and Kevin Rowlette, who made sure that I would not have to endure the next Cat 5 hurricane on my own, along with the others from my local community who helped me make myself useful in the immediate aftermath. Brittany Meyers, Claudia and Ted Reshetiloff, Val Doan, Sherry Burger, Alexia and Gary Lucas, Kelly Verellen Bennett, Sean Laming, Levi James, Lisa Marguiles, Nick Manos—for the warm embrace and soft landing...

I am often asked what was the biggest lesson I learned from the storms, and I've had different answers at different times, but the one overriding lesson of all is: Don't Go It Alone! So, I knew, too, that I would not be able to deliver this work in the world unless I was surrounded by a great team. I was so fortunate to be gifted with the shared vision and support of the very best team of people one could ever hope for—John Willig, who lovingly guided me to step outside of my own process to create something that might actually benefit my readers and who worked indefatigably to find its home with Meg Gibbons, who simply Got It, and enveloped me in her unrelenting embrace and support of this work, helping give me confidence to keep working to make it better for you, my readers. Both of you and the rest of the team at Sourcebooks brought out the best of me and took my vision beyond anything I could have imagined or done on my own.

And to the countless unnamed others of you who have helped me weather the storms in my life, it is not overstating to say that without you, I would not be here today—I am so humbly grateful.

ABOUT THE
AUTHOR

CHRISTINE PERAKIS, ESQ., is a business growth architect, combining her business growth, legal, and entrepreneurial expertise to scale businesses from zero to eight figures in record time by providing comprehensive 360-degree services to support entrepreneurs to grow multimillion-dollar businesses across five continents, while also serving as a one-hundred-ton professional boat captain, speaker, and bestselling author.

From a lucrative legal practice in the entertainment industry over a couple of decades, Christine has partnered with some of her clients in businesses because of their desire to fully utilize her breadth of skills and experience. Consequently, Christine has run or been a part of a management team in ten businesses, achieving results beyond the expectations of all involved, including, most notably, as Chief Operating Officer, taking her company from a 100 percent equity-funded start-up to a ten-million-dollar-a-year business in just a few short years.

Simply put, Christine is passionate about growing businesses and leaders and creating millionaires from an unrelenting pursuit of success.

Christine's first book, *The Entrepreneur's Essential Roadmap*, was a bestselling small business survival guide. She has written for *USA Today*, *Inc.* magazine, and *Bust* magazine, and has also appeared in the *New*

York *Times*, the *Washington Post*, ABC Bloomberg, PBS, ITV, CTV, and myriad nationally syndicated radio and podcast programs globally, among others.

Christine's guiding principle in business and in life has always been:

Weathering the storm to reach a destination requires the partnership of a talented captain and an experienced navigator.

Little did Christine know that she would endure the most cataclysmic storm she would ever encounter alone in her home in Tortola, British Virgin Islands. She developed her Category 5 leadership strategies, programs, and talks while drawing from her experiences to prepare clients to weather any storm. As a speaker, she navigates her audiences through the Category 5–level events in life and business.

To better serve a broad section of small business clients, Christine also offers an online business advisory platform to facilitate small business growth.

Among her other activities, Christine is a success

coach on the advisory board of Elite Hathaway and a mentor to tech start-ups at the prestigious Silicon Beach SAM Preccelerator. She frequently offers her Category 5 leadership workshops and other business growth content to senior leaders in transition within the media, entertainment, and technology spaces. Christine is an avid yacht-racer and former world champion in international pro circuit racing, racing competitively with some of the top professional sailors in the world. Christine was also a professional ski, sailing, and yoga instructor, a volunteer with the National Ski Patrol, and a licensed Emergency Medical Technician for many years.

NEW! Only from Simple Truths®

IGNITE READS
spark impact in just one hour

IGNITE READS IS A NEW SERIES OF 1-HOUR READS WRITTEN BY WORLD-RENOWNED EXPERTS!

These captivating books will help you become the best version of yourself, allowing for new opportunities in your personal and professional life. Accelerate your career and expand your knowledge with these powerful books written on today's hottest ideas.

TRENDING BUSINESS AND PERSONAL GROWTH TOPICS

 Read in an hour or less

 Leading experts and authors

 Bold design and captivating content

EXCLUSIVELY AVAILABLE ON SIMPLETRUTHS.COM

Need a training framework?
Engage your team with discussion guides and PowerPoints for training events or meetings.

Want your own branded editions?
Express gratitude, appreciation, and instill positive perceptions to staff or clients by adding your organization's logo to your edition of the book.

Add a supplemental visual experience
to any meeting, training, or event.

Contact us for special corporate discounts!
(800) 900-3427 x247 or simpletruths@sourcebooks.com

LOVED WHAT YOU READ AND WANT MORE?

Sign up today and be the FIRST to receive advance copies of Simple Truths® NEW releases written and signed by expert authors. Enjoy a complete package of supplemental materials that can help you host or lead a successful event. This high-value program will uplift you to be the best version of yourself!

— SIMPLE TRUTHS —
ELITE CLUB
ONE MONTH. ONE BOOK. ONE HOUR.

Your monthly dose of motivation, inspiration, and personal growth.

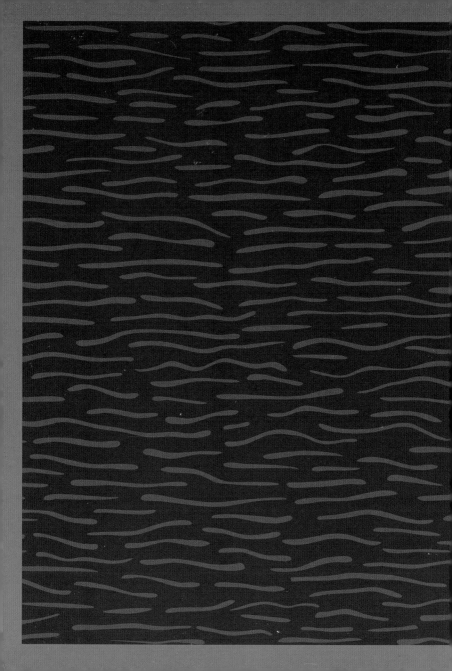